MW01537867

This Book Belongs To

First Name ____________________

Last Name ____________________

Made in the USA
Las Vegas, NV
06 January 2021

15304054R00072